GRANDMA'S
Album

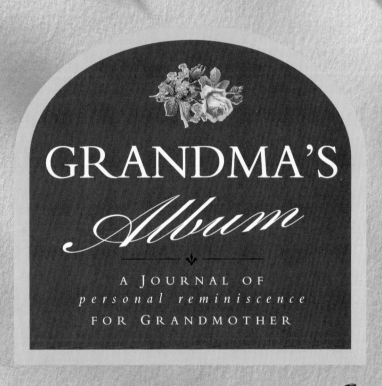

GRANDMA'S
Album

A JOURNAL OF
personal reminiscence
FOR GRANDMOTHER

SIMON & SCHUSTER

LONDON · SYDNEY · NEW YORK · TOKYO · SINGAPORE · TORONTO

Designed, written and edited by
BRIDGEWATER BOOKS LTD

COMPILED AND WRITTEN BY JOANNA JESSOP

Designed by Peter Bridgewater

Edited by Viv Croot

Photography by Guy Ryecart

Illustrated by Lorraine Harrison

Typesetting by Vanessa Good

Prop Research by Jane Lanaway / Annie Moss

CLB 3307

This edition published 1995 by Simon & Schuster

© CLB Publishing, Godalming, Surrey

All rights reserved

Colour separations by Scantrans PTE Ltd, Singapore

Printed and bound in Italy

ISBN 0-671-71438-4

ONTENTS

THIS ALBUM is designed to help a grandmother tell her story. It is set out in sections that serve as general guidelines for recalling and recording family history, earliest childhood memories, scenes from family life and the birth and growth of children and grandchildren. There are special sections to record important dates and to give brief descriptions of special events and family milestones. The general theme of each page is reflected in the readings and photographs – images that are designed to help elicit memories of past people, places and events. The Album also includes sections for favourite photographs and precious mementos, as well as favourite recipes, household hints and general advice that will be a treasure to future generations.

The first forty years of life furnish the text, while the remaining thirty supply the commentary.

. . . .

ARTUR
SCHOPENHAUER
(1788–1860)

6

> Life is a country
> the old have seen
> and lived in.
> Those who have to
> travel through it can
> only learn the way
> from them.
>
> . . . .
>
> ANONYMOUS

Grandma's Album is a summing up of life's experience –
a reflection on the past in the light of the serenity and
wisdom that comes with maturity. It is a chance to
capture those amusing and touching anecdotes of days
gone by, which if not recorded will be lost forever.
It is a grandmother's gift to the future. But most
of all, Grandma's Album is a chance to relive
and delight in the details of the past.

 FAMILY HISTORY

> Every man is an omnibus in which his ancestors ride.
>
> . . . .
>
> OLIVER
> WENDELL HOLMES
> (1809–1894)

OUR ANCESTORS are lost to the past unless someone makes a record of their lives and deeds. The "Family History" section of this Album is where you can design a family tree that shows the relationships among all your ancestors as far back as you can remember, with dates of births, marriages and deaths. In addition to the facts, you may want to record some aspects of your family's history: where they came from; how they made a living; any special events or achievements. It is also interesting to recall any fascinating titbits they may have passed on to you about their lives – for example, the attitudes and fashions of their day, how they entertained themselves, how they viewed world events. It is this kind of everyday detail that brings the past alive.

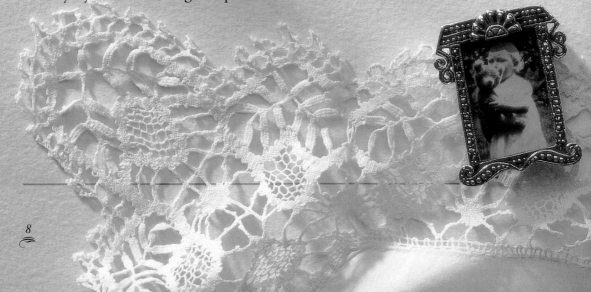

One always
retains the traces of
one's origin.
. . . .

ERNEST RENAN
(1823–1892)

Family History

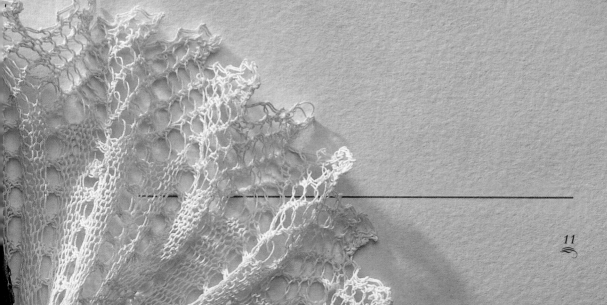

The brave are
born from the brave
and good.

. . . .

HORACE
(65–8 B.C.)

The past is a
foreign country:
they do things
differently there.

. . . .

L. P. HARTLEY
(1895–1972)

RECOLLECTIONS

EVENTS FROM OUR PAST form the fabric of our lives. Everyone's life is a mixture of good times and bad times, of highs and lows, which stand out when we remember the past. It is easier to see the pattern of life's events when viewed from a distance and to understand how our experiences have made us what we are.

This section of the album is for recording your personal history, starting with your earliest recollections of family life and childhood. This is your opportunity to describe what the world was like as you were growing up and what were the major influences in your youth, to remember your friends and schoolmates and to tell of your experiences of becoming a woman and a wife.

> Underneath the surface of Today Lies Yesterday, and what we call the Past, The only thing which never can decay.
>
> . . . .
>
> EUGENE LEE–HAMILTON (1845–1907)

Our deeds still travel
with us from afar,
And what we
have been makes us
what we are.

. . . .

GEORGE ELIOT
(1819–1880)

Who ran to help me,
when I fell,
And would some
pretty story tell,
Or kiss the place to
make it well?
My Mother.

. . . .

ANN TAYLOR
(1782–1866)

I remember,
I remember
How my childhood
fleeted by,
The mirth of its
December,
And the warmth
of its July.

W. M. PRAED
(1802–1839)

Sweet childish days,
that were as long
As twenty days
are now.
. . . .
WILLIAM
WORDSWORTH
(1770–1850)

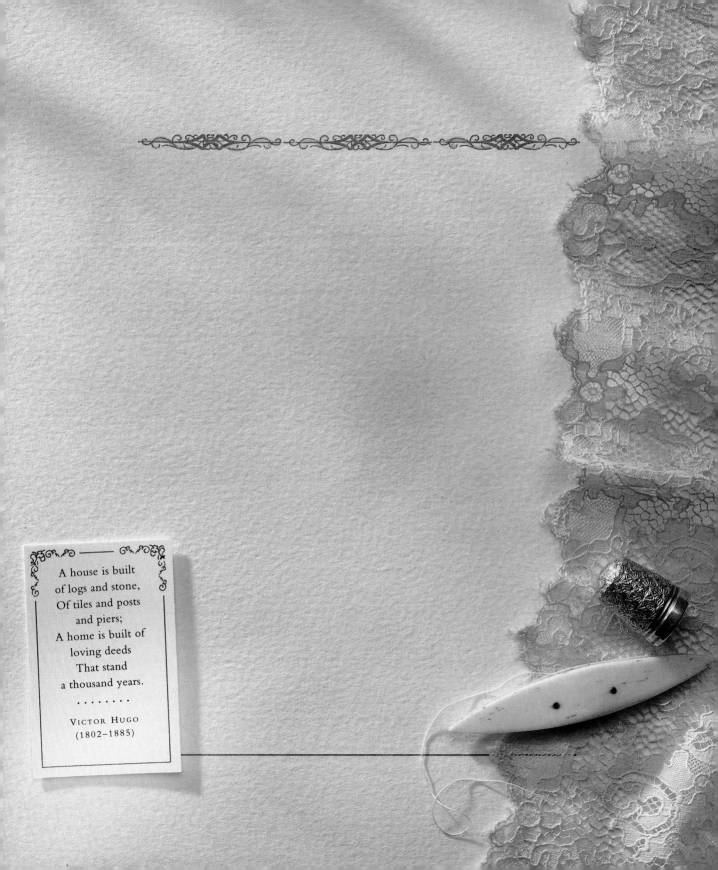

A house is built
of logs and stone,
Of tiles and posts
and piers;
A home is built of
loving deeds
That stand
a thousand years.

. . . .

VICTOR HUGO
(1802–1885)

> Oh be thou blest
> with all that heav'n
> can send,
> Long Health, long
> Youth, long Pleasure
> and a Friend....
>
> . . . .
>
> Alexander Pope
> (1688–1744)

From quiet homes
and first beginning,
Out to the
undiscovered ends,
There's nothing worth
the wear of winning,
But laughter and the
love of friends.
· · · · · · · ·
HILAIRE BELLOC
(1870–1953) ·

> Education is an admirable thing, but it is well to remember from time to time that nothing worth knowing can be taught.
>
> · · · · · · · ·
>
> OSCAR WILDE
> (1854–1900)

The more we study
the more we discover
our ignorance.

· · · · · · · ·

PERCY
BYSSHE SHELLEY
(1792–1822)

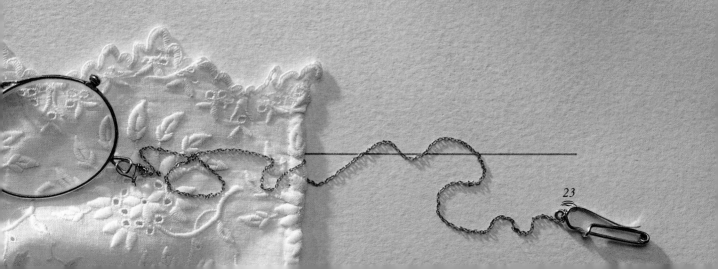

Fashions, after all,
are only induced
epidemics.

. . . .

GEORGE
BERNARD SHAW
(1856–1950)

> Every age has its
> pleasures, its style of
> wit, and its own ways.
>
> . . . .
>
> NICOLAS
> BOILEAU-DESPREAUX
> (1636–1711)

> It was the best
> of times,
> it was the worst
> of times, it was the age
> of wisdom,
> it was the age
> of foolishness.
>
> . . . .
>
> CHARLES DICKENS
> (1812–1870)

> The web of our life
> is a mingled yarn,
> good and ill together.
>
> . . . .
>
> WILLIAM
> SHAKESPEARE
> (1564–1616)

Happiness is
beneficial to the body,
but it is grief
that develops the soul.

. . . .

MARCEL PROUST
(1871–1922)

29

When a small
child ... I thought
that success spelled
happiness.
I was wrong.
Happiness is like a
butterfly which
appears and delights
us for one
brief moment, but
soon flits away.

ANNA PAVLOVA
(1881–1931)

But all that I could
think of, in the
darkness and the cold,
Was just that I
was leaving home and
my folks
were growing old.

. . . .

ROBERT
LOUIS STEVENSON
(1850–1894)

Work banishes three
great evils:
boredom, vice and
poverty.

. . . .

FRANCOIS-MARIE
VOLTAIRE
(1694–1778)

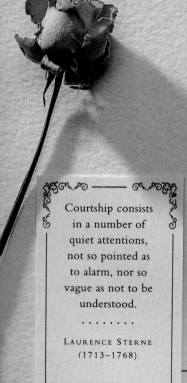

Courtship consists
in a number of
quiet attentions,
not so pointed as
to alarm, nor so
vague as not to be
understood.

. . . .

LAURENCE STERNE
(1713–1768)

Strephon's kiss
was lost in jest,
Robin's lost in play,
But the kiss
in Colin's eyes
Haunts me night
and day.

. . . .

SARA TEASDALE
(1884–1933)

_____

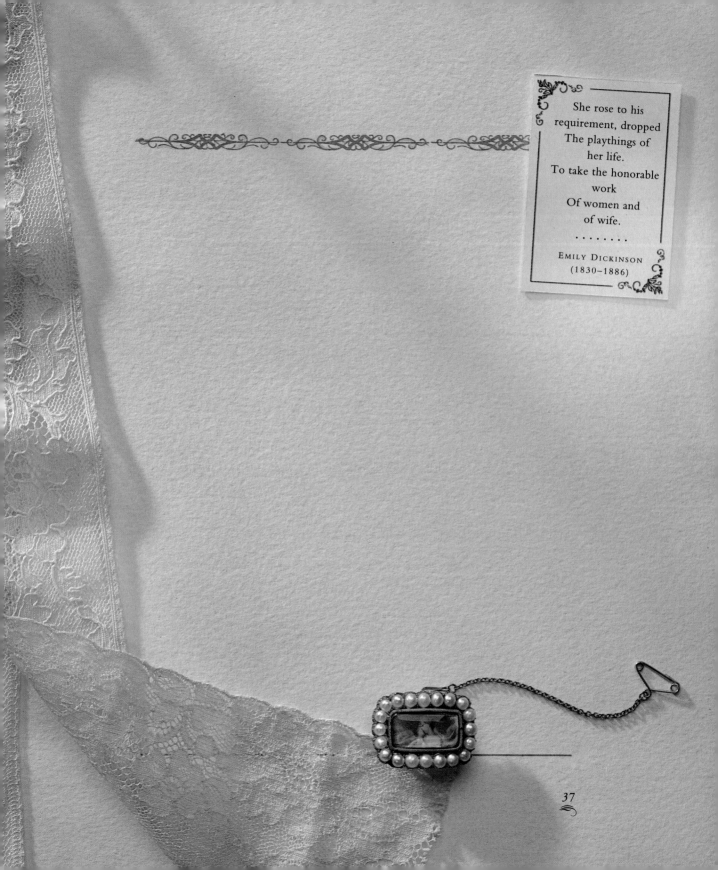

She rose to his
requirement, dropped
The playthings of
her life.
To take the honorable
work
Of women and
of wife.
. . . .

EMILY DICKINSON
(1830–1886)

My Children

THE MOTHERHOOD years are full of special memories. A new life enters into your keeping, to protect and guide through childhood and to prepare for the demands of the world. Here is a chance to recall some of those precious moments — the happiness and mishaps, the joys and sorrows — as the infants you brought into the world grew and developed into children and became adults with lives of their own.

Youth fades;
love droops;
the leaves
of friendship fall:
A mother's secret love
outlives them all.

· · · · · · · ·

OLIVER
WENDELL HOLMES
(1809–1894)

Your children
are not your children.
They are the sons
and daughters of
Life's longing for itself.
They come
through you
but not from you.
And though they are
with you yet
they belong not to you

· · · · · · · ·

KAHLIL GIBRAN
(1833–1931)

My Children ❖ *Births*

Babies are bits
of star-dust blown
from the hand of God.
Lucky the woman
who knows
the pangs of birth for
she has held a star.

. . . .

LARRY BARRETTO
(1890–?)

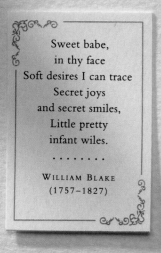

Sweet babe,
in thy face
Soft desires I can trace
Secret joys
and secret smiles,
Little pretty
infant wiles.

· · · · · · · ·

WILLIAM BLAKE
(1757–1827)

A babe in the
house
is a well-spring of
pleasure.
. . . .

MARTIN F. TUPPER
(1810–1889)

My Children ❖ *As Toddlers*

The greatest poem
ever known
Is one all poets have
outgrown:
The poetry innate,
untold,
Of being only
four years old.

· · · · · · · ·

CHRISTOPHER
MORLEY
(1890–1957)

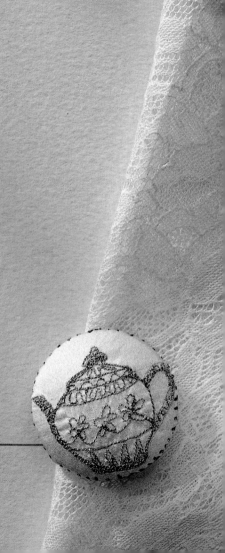

Small children
have a habit of
conferring persistent
youth upon
their parents, and by
their eager vitality
postpone the
unenterprising
cautions and timidities
of middle age.

. . . .

VERA BRITTAIN
(1896–1970)

How pleasant is
Saturday night,
When I've tried all the
week to be good,
Not spoken a word
that is bad,
And obliged everyone
that I could.

. . . .

Nancy
Dennis Sproat
(1766–1826)

MY CHILDREN ❖ *Ambitions and Achievements*

How beautiful
is youth!
how bright it gleams
With its illusions,
aspirations, dreams!

· · · · · · · ·

HENRY WADSWORTH
LONGFELLOW
(1807–1882)

If children grew up
according to early
indications, we
should have nothing
but geniuses.

· · · · · · · ·

JOHANN WOLFGANG
VON GOETHE
(1749–1832)

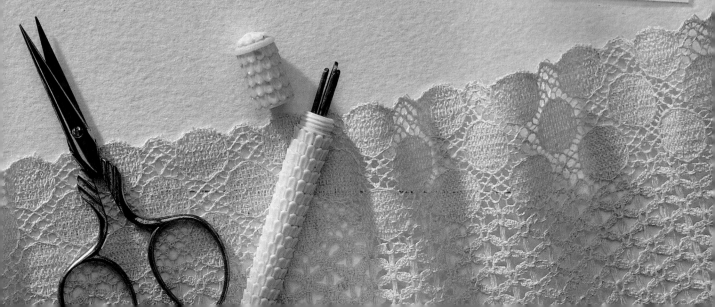

52

The child she
had learned to love
had vanished somehow
and here was this tall,
serious-eyed girl of
fifteen, with the
thoughtful brows and
the proudly poised
little head, in her
place. Marilla loved
the girl as much as she
had loved the child,
but she was conscious
of a queer, sorrowful
sense of loss.

. . . .

L. M. MONTGOMERY
(1874–1942)

Quite suddenly,
too, I realised ...
that the inevitable
clash between the
generations
diminishes, also
inevitably, with the
passing of the years.

. . . .

VERA BRITTAIN
(1896–1970)

Blessed is he who
has found his work;
let him ask for
no other blessedness.

. . . .

THOMAS CARLYLE
(1795–1881)

But happy they!
The happiest
of their kind!
Whom gentle stars
unite, and in one fate
Their hearts, their
fortunes, and their
being blend.

. . . .

JAMES THOMSON
(1834–1882)

BECOMING A GRANDMOTHER

BECOMING A GRANDMOTHER is like having a second chance at motherhood, but with more space to stand back and enjoy. Perhaps it is because grandmothers move a little slower that they have time for their grandchildren in a way that busy parents never do. It is a grandmother's privilege to read those special fairy tales, to answer those pressing questions such as why the sky is blue, to surprise with gifts of sweets and small delights and, best of all, to entertain with stories of their parents as young children – stories that every grandchild loves to hear. In your grandchildren you can relive the good times you had with your own children. As your grandchildren grow and develop, it is a joy to see the family traits and resemblances being reborn in a new generation.

This section of the Album is for recording your feelings and reactions on becoming a grandmother. Here, too, you can provide an account of each grandchild's development over the years. You can write about those momentous events, such as your grandchild's first words, and about those special times you had together.

The first time
I held my grandchild
was a joy
beyond compare.
The child of my child.
I felt I was looking at
my own mortality.

. . . .

A GRANDMOTHER

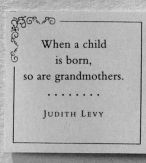

> When a child
> is born,
> so are grandmothers.
> . . . .
>
> JUDITH LEVY

Where did you
come from baby dear?
Out of the Everywhere
into the here ....

· · · · · · · ·

GEORGE MACDONALD
(1824–1905)

He smiles and clasps
his tiny hands,
With sunbeams o'er
him gleaming,
A world of
baby fairyland
He visits while he's
dreaming.

. . . .

JOSEPH
ASHBY-STERRY
(1838–1917)

What are
little boys made of?
Frogs and snails and
puppy-dogs' tails,
That's what little boys
are made of.
What are
little girls made of ?
Sugar and spice and
all things nice,
That's what little girls
are made of.

. . . .

TRADITIONAL

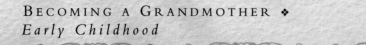

BECOMING A GRANDMOTHER ❖
Early Childhood

It is the season
now to go
About the country
high and low,
Among the lilacs
hand in hand,
And two by two
in fairy land.
· · · · · · · ·
ROBERT
LOUIS STEVENSON
(1850–1894)

Babies do not want
to hear about babies
they like to be told
of giants and castles
and of somewhat
which can
stretch and stimulate
their little minds.

· · · · · · · ·

SAMUEL JOHNSON
(1709–1784)

> "The time
> has come,"
> the Walrus said,
> "To talk of
> many things:
> Of shoes — and ships —
> and sealing wax —
> Of cabbages —
> and kings —
> And why the sea is
> boiling hot —
> And whether
> pigs have wings."
>
> · · · · · · ·
>
> LEWIS CARROLL
> (1832–1898)

Becoming a Grandmother ❖
When the Grandchildren Come to Visit

_____

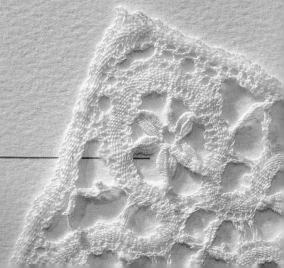

Grandma Gurney
Gives to me
Gooseberry tart
And hot sweet tea.

She sits up high
On her rocking chair
She can't touch
the floor
But she doesn't care.
. . . .

A.E. Dudley

I love spoiling
my grandchildren.
I send them back
home to their parents
dirty and tired
and full of sweets.
And best of all,
I don't have to pay
the consequences.
. . . .
A GRANDMOTHER

Spending time with
my grandchildren
is like recapturing my
youth. I have the
time and patience
that I didn't have
as a mother to answer
their questions, read
their stories and play
their games.

· · · · · · · · ·

A Grandmother

Granny Granny
please comb my hair
you always
take your time
you always
take such care

· · · · · · · ·

Grace Nichols

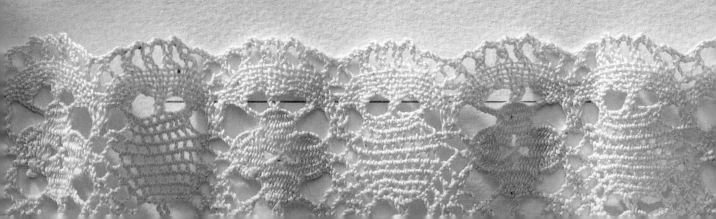

One afternoon a
sound came out of her
house like jets taking
off, her grandson
practising his guitar.
She was there, knitting,
rocking saying
to him ...
Kevin didn't hear a
word she said, and she
didn't know the
music was blowing her
hair back.

. . . .

A GRANDMOTHER

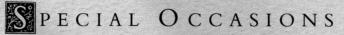SPECIAL OCCASIONS

EVERY FAMILY has its own special occasions and events that bring everyone together and strengthen the family bonds. Over the years, some special occasions, such as New Year's celebrations, wedding anniversaries or birthdays, take on the trappings of a family tradition in which certain customs and routines are followed. These annual affairs mark the passing years. But any occasion that is

The holiest of holidays are those Kept by ourselves in silence and apart; The secret anniversaries of the heart, When the full tide of feeling overflows; The happy days unclouded to their close.

· · · · · · · ·

HENRY WADSWORTH LONGFELLOW (1807–1882)

remembered with fondness is special. A trip to the countryside or a picnic in the park can bring as much joy to a family as the most elaborate festivity. All these events – the weddings, graduations, family outings and get-togethers – are an important part of a family's history. But also important, although perhaps significant to you alone, are those special quiet moments, the "secret anniversaries of the heart".

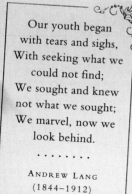

Our youth began
with tears and sighs,
With seeking what we
could not find;
We sought and knew
not what we sought;
We marvel, now we
look behind.

· · · · · · · ·

ANDREW LANG
(1844–1912)

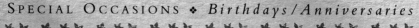

The ring so worn as
you behold,
So thin, so pale,
is yet of gold:
The passion such
it was to prove:
Worn with life's cares,
love yet was love.

. . . .

GEORGE CRABBE
(1754–1832)

'Tis forty years since
we were wed;
We are ailing and grey
needs not be said;
But Willie's eyes are
as blue an' soft
As the day when he
wooed me in
father's croft.

. . . .

ROBERT BRIDGES
(1844–1930)

They are not long
the days
of wine and roses:
Out of a misty dream
Our path emerges
for a while, then closes
Within a dream.

· · · · · · · ·

ERNEST DOWSON
(1867–1900)

Learn to make
the most of life,
Lose no happy day,
Time will never bring
thee back
Chances swept away!
Leave no tender
word unsaid,
Love while love
shall last;
"The mill cannot grind
With water that
is past."

SARAH DOUDNEY
(1843–1926)

My mother groan'd,
my father wept,
Into the dangerous
world I leapt;
Helpless, naked,
piping loud,
Like a fiend hid in
a cloud.

· · · · · · · ·

WILLIAM BLAKE
(1757–1827)

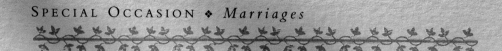

It is a truth universally
acknowledged,
that a single man in
possession of a good
fortune, must be in
want of a wife.

· · · · · · · ·

JANE AUSTEN
(1775–1817)

But oh for the
touch of
a vanished hand,
And the sound
of a voice that is still!
• • • • • • • •
ALFRED,
LORD TENNYSON
(1809–1892)

For all pairs
of lovers without
exception, bereavement
is a universal and
integral part of our
experience of love.
It follows marriage as
normally as marriage
follows courtship
or as autumn
follows summer.

· · · · · · ·

C. S. LEWIS
(1898–1963)

FAMILY MILESTONES

MILESTONES ARE THE SIGNIFICANT EVENTS that occur in the passage through life. They include the births, marriages and deaths of family members. Your family may have its own personal milestones, such as starting a new job, or moving to a new house or a new town, that marked a major change in the course of your lives. In these next few pages you may want to make a record of your family milestones.

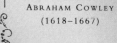

This I know
without being told,
'Tis time to live as I
grow old.
'Tis time short
pleasures now to take,
Of little Life
the best to make,
And manage wisely
the last stake.

. . . .

ABRAHAM COWLEY
(1618–1667)

Family Milestones

All my past life is
mine no more;
The flying hours
are gone,
Like transitory dreams
given o'er
Whose images are
kept in store
By memory alone.

········

JOHN WILMOT
(1647–1680)

The more we live,
more brief appear
Our life's
succeeding stages;
A day to childhood
seems a year,
A year like
passing ages ...

········

THOMAS CAMPBELL
(1777–1844)

IMPORTANT DATES

THE FOLLOWING PAGES are set aside for recording important dates such as births, marriages and deaths. This record of dates may prove to be a valuable source of information to future generations.

> Life is not dated merely by years. Events are sometimes the best calendars.
>
> . . . .
>
> BENJAMIN DISRAELI
> (1804–1881)

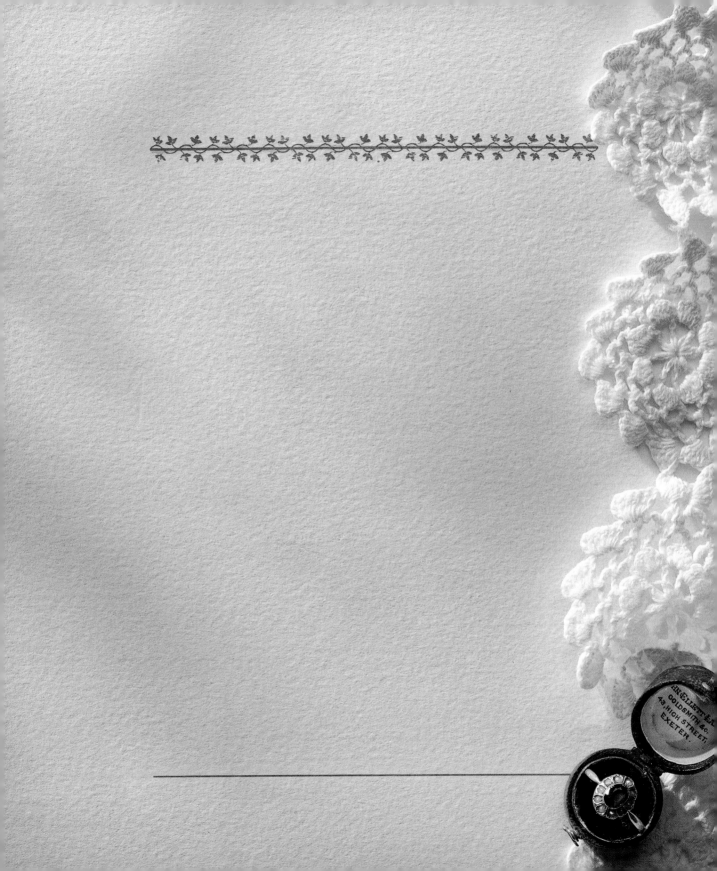

IMPORTANT DATES

> Everything that happens happens as it should, and if you observe carefully, you will find this to be so.
>
> . . . .
>
> MARCUS AURELIUS (121–180)

The wise mind
Mourns less for what
age takes away
Than what it leaves
behind.

· · · · · · · ·

WILLIAM
WORDSWORTH
(1770–1850)

HOLIDAYS & OUTINGS

HOLIDAYS ARE A TIME to step out of the hectic rush of life and take a look at something new. The something new may be an exotic location in a foreign country or it may be a visit to a beauty spot closer to home. The break with routine may be nothing more than a day's outing, a trip to the countryside or to the nearest park. But no matter how exotic or mundane the holiday, it is an adventure shared together as a family. It is an opportunity to relate to each other outside the usual routine of daily life, and perhaps to become re-acquainted with those you love. In the next few pages, you may like to recall some of your favourite and most memorable family holidays and outings.

For my part,
I travel not to go
anywhere, but to go.
I travel for travel's sake.
The great affair
is to move.
. . . .
ROBERT
LOUIS STEVENSON
(1850–1894)

HOLIDAYS & OUTINGS ✦ *Travels*

> I must go down
> to the seas again,
> to the
> vagrant gypsy life ...
>
> · · · · · · · ·
>
> JOHN MASEFIELD
> (1878–1967)

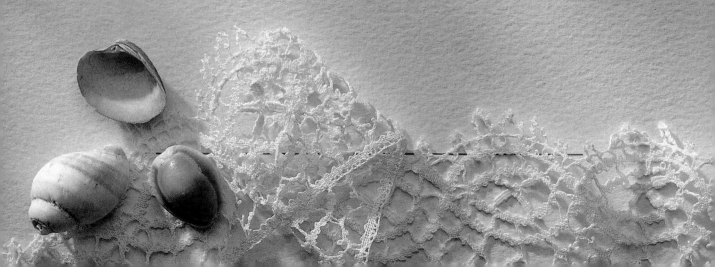

Afoot and
light-hearted I take to
the open road,
Healthy and free, the
world before me,
The long brown path
before me leading
wherever I choose.

. . . .

WALT WHITMAN
(1819–1892)

Holidays & Outings ❖
Trips to the Countryside/at Leisure

To one who has
been long
in the city pent,
'Tis very sweet to look
into the fair
And open face
of heaven....

. . . .

John Keats
(1795–1821)

What is this life if,
full of care,
We have no time
to stand and stare?

. . . .

W.H. Davies
(1871–1940)

Here of a Sunday
morning
My love and
I would lie,
And see
the coloured counties,
And hear
the larks so high
About us in the sky.

· · · · · · · ·

A.E. HOUSMAN
(1850–1936)

The kiss of the
sun for pardon,
The song of the birds
for mirth —
One is nearer
God's Heart
in a garden
Than anywhere else
on earth.
. . . .

DOROTHY GURNEY
(1858–1932)

REUNIONS

THERE IS NO JOY COMPARABLE to the joy of greeting a loved one after a long separation. Then comes the fun of catching up on all the news and the telling and re-telling of all the little things that have happened since you were last together. Reunions with those we love are some of the most delightful moments in life, filled with sweet memories.

Absences are a good
influence in love
and keep it bright and
delicate.
. . . .
ROBERT
LOUIS STEVENSON
(1850–1894)

Love reckons
hours for months,
and days for years;
And every little absence
is an age.

. . . .

JOHN DRYDEN
(1631–1700

FRIENDS & NEIGHBOURS

IT IS INTERESTING TO RECALL the friends and neighbours who played important roles in our lives. In this section of the Album you may want to look back on those people outside the family who hold a prominent place in your memories. There may be interesting anecdotes to relate and reminiscences of times when the trials of life strengthened the bonds of friendship.

Fate chooses your
relatives, you choose
your friends.

· · · · · · · ·

ABBÉ
JACQUES DELILLE
(1738–1813)

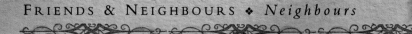

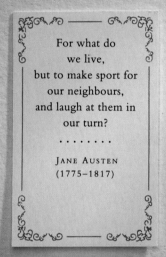

For what do
we live,
but to make sport for
our neighbours,
and laugh at them in
our turn?

· · · · · · · ·

JANE AUSTEN
(1775–1817)

My apple tree
will never get across
And eat the cones
under his pines,
I tell him.
He only says "Good
fences make good
neighbours."

ROBERT FROST
(1874–1963)

Favourite Photographs

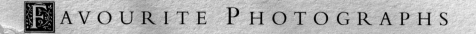

THE FOLLOWING PAGES of the Album are set aside for your favourite photographs. Here, the images of the people and places that feature in your recollections of the past can be gathered together for safe keeping.

For it is pleasure, too, to remember.

· · · · · · · ·

OVID
(43 B.C.–17 A.D.)

O there are
voices of the Past,
Link of a broken chain,
Wings that can
bear me back to Times
Which cannot
come again,
Yet God forbid
that I should lose
The echoes that remain!

· · · · · · · · ·

ADELAIDE ANN
PROCTOR
(1825–1864)

Favourite Photographs

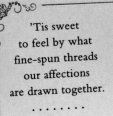

'Tis sweet
to feel by what
fine-spun threads
our affections
are drawn together.

. . . .

LAWRENCE STERNE
(1713–1768)

The past is ours,
and there we have all
who loved us,
and whom we love as
much as ever,
ay, more than ever.

. . . .

MAX MÜLLER
(1823–1900)

No Spring,
nor Summer beauty
hath such grace,
As I have seen in one
autumnal face.

· · · · · · · ·

JOHN DONNE
(1572–1631)

Our hearts
are young
'neath wrinkled rind:
Life more amusing
than we thought.
· · · · · · ·
ANDREW LANG
(1844–1912)

Favourite Photographs

No past
is dead for us,
but only
sleeping, Love.

. . . .

HELEN
HUNT JACKSON
(1831–1885)

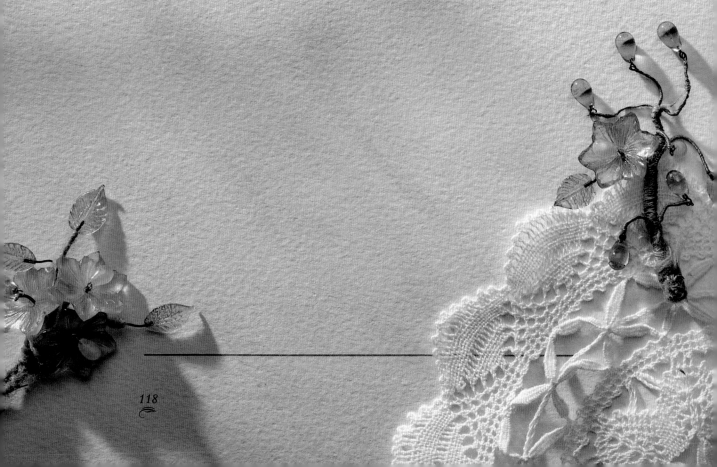

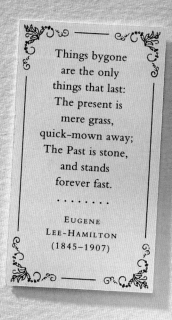

Things bygone
are the only
things that last:
The present is
mere grass,
quick-mown away;
The Past is stone,
and stands
forever fast.

· · · · · · · ·

EUGENE
LEE-HAMILTON
(1845–1907)

Favourite Photographs

I cannot think
of them as dead,
Who walk with me
no more;
Along the path of life
I tread –
They have but gone
before.

· · · · · · · ·

FREDERICK
L. HOSMER
(1840–1929)

> Youth
> having passed,
> there is nothing to lose
> but memory.
> Cherishing the past
> without regrets
> and viewing the future
> without misgivings,
> we wait, then,
> for nightfall when one
> may rest and call
> it a life.
>
> . . . .
>
> GEORGE MACDONALD
> (1824–1905)

When you are old
and full of sleep,
And nodding by the
fire, take down
this book,
And slowly read, and
dream of the soft look
Your eyes had once,
and of their shadows
deep...
· · · · · · · ·
W.B. YEATS
(1865–1939)

MEMORABILIA

SOME TRIFLING THING may be more valuable in sentiment than all the riches in the world. A love letter, a lock of baby hair, a child's first Mother's Day card made specially for you, a wedding invitation – all these things are filled with precious memories. In this section of the Album you can assemble the mementos of the past, those simple things that bring such joy.

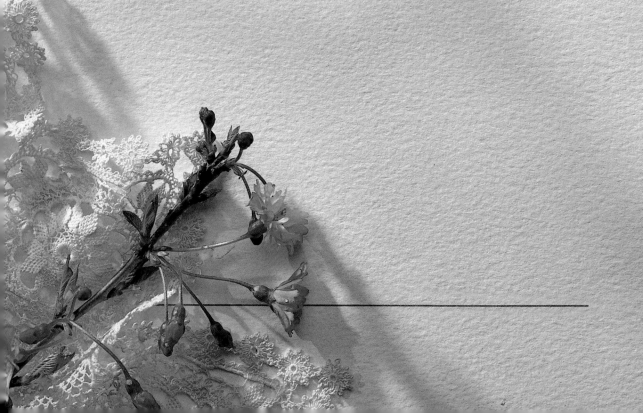

Who hath not saved
some trifling thing
More prized than
jewel rare,
A faded flower,
a broken ring,
A tress of golden hair.
. . . .
ELLEN
CLEMENTINE HOWARTH
(1827–1899)

MEMORABILIA

I love it, I love it;
and who shall dare
To chide me
for loving that old
arm-chair.

. . . .

ELIZA COOK
(1818–1889)

I love everything
that's old;
old friends, old times,
old manners,
old books, old wines.
. . . .
OLIVER GOLDSMITH
(1728–1774)

MEMORABILIA

All beauteous things
for which we live
By laws of time and
space decay.
But Oh, the very
reason why
I clasp them, is
because they die.
. . . .
WILLIAM CORY
(1823–1892)

Teach us delight in
simple things,
And mirth that has no
bitter springs.
. . . .
RUDYARD KIPLING
(1865–1936)

A thing of beauty
is a joy for ever:
Its loveliness increases;
it will never
Pass into nothingness.

. . . .

JOHN KEATS
(1795–1821)

Ah, we fondly cherish
Faded things
That had better perish.
Memory clings
To each leaf it saves.

. . . .

J.H. BONER
(1845–1903)

When Time, who
steals our years away,
Shall steal our
pleasures too,
The mem'ry of the past
will stay,
And half our joy renew.

· · · · · · · ·

THOMAS MOORE
(1799–1845)

Better by far
you should forget
and smile
Than that you
should remember and
be sad.

· · · · · · · ·

CHRISTINA ROSSETTI
(1830–1874)

MEMORABILIA

And memories
vague of
half-forgotten things,
Not true or false,
but sweet
to think upon.

· · · · · · · ·

WILLIAM MORRIS
(1834–1896)

'Tis but a little
faded flower,
But oh,
how fondly dear!
'Twill bring me back
one golden hour,
Through many
a weary year.

· · · · · · · ·

ELLEN
CLEMENTINE HOWARTH
(1827–1899)

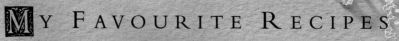

My Favourite Recipes

E VERY WOMAN has her favourite recipes; usually the best of these cannot be found in any cookbook. They may have been passed down from mother to daughter over the generations, changing and adapting along the way. Or they may be particular favourites devised for your children. Often only you know the exact ingredients and proportions, although the rest of the family are familiar with the delicious results.

Here is an opportunity to write down your favourite recipes for the benefit of future cooks.

> I feel a recipe
> is only a theme,
> which an intelligent
> cook can play
> each time with
> a variation.
> . . . .
> MADAME BENOIT

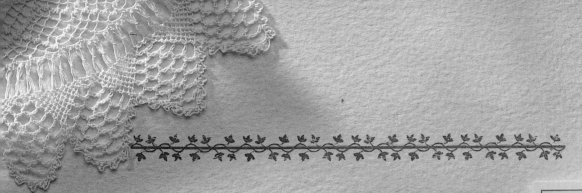

There is no love
sincerer than
the love of food.
. . . .
GEORGE
BERNARD SHAW
(1856–1950)

MY FAVOURITE RECIPES

> The way to
> a man's heart is
> through his stomach.
> . . . .
> FANNIE FERN
> (1811–1872)

Kissing don't last;
cookery do!

. . . .

GEORGE MEREDITH
(1812–1909)

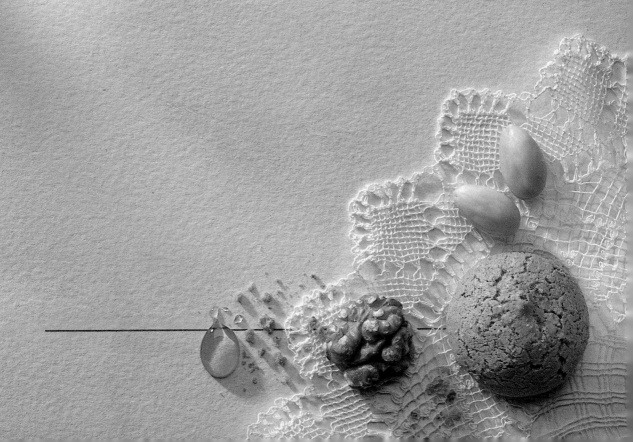

My Favourite Recipes

If you wish
to grow thinner,
diminish your dinner,
And take to light claret
instead of pale ale;
Look down
with utter contempt
upon butter,
And never touch bread
till it's toasted —
or stale.

. . . .

H. S. LEIGH
(1837–1883)

My Favourite Recipes

They dined
on mince,
and slices of quince,
Which they ate
with a runcible spoon;
And hand in hand,
on the edge
of the sand,
They danced by the
light of the moon.

. . . .

EDWARD LEAR
(1812–1880)

Old age and
the wear of time
teach many things.

· · · · · · · ·

SOPHOCLES
(495–406 B.C.)

ONE OF THE REWARDS of growing older is the accumulation of wisdom along the way. Every woman who has run a household and raised a family has a wealth of valuable information and good advice to pass on. This last section of Grandma's Album is to capture the pearls of wisdom that the years have taught you.

Cleaning your house
while your kids
are still growing
is like shovelling
the walk before
it stops snowing.

. . . .

PHYLLIS DILLER

> Man's work lasts
> till the set of sun;
> Woman's work
> is never done.
>
> . . . .
>
> ANONYMOUS

Whatever
women do
they must do twice
as well as men
to be thought half
as good.
Luckily,
this is not difficult.
. . . .
CHARLOTTE WHITTON

Annual income
twenty pounds,
annual expenditure
nineteen nineteen six,
result happiness.
Annual income
twenty pounds,
annual expenditure
twenty pounds ought
and six,
result misery.

· · · · · · · ·

CHARLES DICKENS
(1812–1870)

I long to accomplish
a great and noble task,
but it is my chief duty
to accomplish small
tasks as if they were
great and noble.

. . . .

HELEN KELLER
(1880–1968)

151

❖ ACKOWLEDGEMENTS ❖

Grateful acknowledgement is given for permission to reprint the copyright material in this book.

HILAIRE BELLOC: excerpt from "From Quiet Homes" from *Complete Verse* by Hilaire Belloc and published by Pimlico by permission of Peters, Fraser and Dunlop Group Ltd.

VERA BRITTAIN: excerpts from "Testament of Youth" by Vera Brittain are included with the permission of Paul Berry, her literary executor, Victor Gollancz Ltd., and Virago Press.

A. E. DUDLEY: "Grandma Gurney" by permission of the author.

ROBERT FROST: excerpt from "Mending Wall" from *The Poetry of Robert Frost* edited by Edward Connery Lathem, by permission of Random Century Ltd., on behalf of the Estate of Robert Frost.

C. S. LEWIS: excerpt from Grief Observed published by Faber and Faber Ltd., by permission of the publisher.

JOHN MASEFIELD: excerpts from "Sea Fever" and "Growing Old" by permission of The Society of Authors as the literary representatives of the Estate of John Masefield.

The publisher has endeavoured to trace all copyright holders for material in this journal but apologizes for any inadvertent omissions, which will be rectified in any reprint.

Special thanks are given to the following, for their kind and generous help in supplying photographic props

Anna Lise Clarke ❖ *Grannies Attic* ❖ *Paul Goble*
Vanessa Good ❖ *Lorraine Harrison* ❖ *Home Sweet Home*
Peter Hopkins ❖ *Rose Hopkins* ❖ *Rosemary Lanaway*
Christine Marr ❖ *Priscilla McIntosh* ❖ *Moyra Moody*
Margaret Moss ❖ *Karen Ryecart* ❖ *Mike Skinner*